REAL MONSTERS

GIANT CENTIPEDE

COLOSSAL CREEPER OF THE NIGHT

PAIGE V. POLINSKY

Checkerboard
Library

An Imprint of Abdo Publishing
abdopublishing.com

ABDOPUBLISHING.COM

Published by Abdo Publishing, a division of ABDO, PO Box 398166, Minneapolis, Minnesota 55439. Copyright © 2017 by Abdo Consulting Group, Inc. International copyrights reserved in all countries. No part of this book may be reproduced in any form without written permission from the publisher. Checkerboard Library™ is a trademark and logo of Abdo Publishing.

Printed in the United States of America, North Mankato, Minnesota
092016
012017

THIS BOOK CONTAINS
RECYCLED MATERIALS

Design: Christa Schneider, Mighty Media, Inc.
Production: Mighty Media, Inc.
Editor: Rebecca Felix
Cover Photo: Shutterstock Images
Interior Photos: Animal Demography Unit/Department of Biological Sciences, University of Cape Town, p. 23; Dima Korol, p. 27; Getty Images, pp. 13, 19, 25; iStockphoto, p. 17; Melvyn Yeo, p. 15; Mighty Media, Inc., pp. 7, 21; Shutterstock Images, pp. 4-5, 6, 7, 11, 29; Wikimedia Commons, p. 9

Publisher's Cataloging-in-Publication Data
Names: Polinsky, Paige V., author.
Title: Giant centipede : colossal creeper of the night / by Paige V. Polinsky.
Other titles: Colossal creeper of the night
Description: Minneapolis, MN : Abdo Publishing, 2017. | Series: Real monsters | Includes bibliographical references and index.
Identifiers: LCCN 2016944862 | ISBN 9781680784183 (lib. bdg.) | ISBN 9781680797718 (ebook)
Subjects: LCSH: Centipedes--Juvenile literature.
Classification: DDC 595.6/2--dc23
LC record available at http://lccn.loc.gov/2016944862

CONTENTS

Deep in the jungle, dozens of legs scuttle across the ground. A glossy shell shines in the moonlight. The creature slithers over the earth, antennae waving. This giant centipede is on the hunt.

The centipede enters a dark cave. It creeps up the stony wall and onto the cave's ceiling. It uses several back legs to grip to the ceiling. Its front half dangles midair. The trap is set.

Several bats soon fly toward the cave's exit. One crashes into the hanging hunter. The centipede INJECTS it with VENOM. The bat becomes a feast for the world's strangest centipede.

CREATURE FEATURE

NAME: Giant centipede

NICKNAMES: Amazonian giant centipede, Peruvian giant yellow-leg centipede, death crawler

CLASS: Chilopoda

SIZE: 10 to 12 inches (25 to 31 cm) long

COLORATION: Dark red and black body, orange or yellow legs

LIFE SPAN: About 10 years

MONSTROUS CHARACTERISTICS

> Massive size

> Dozens of legs

> **Venomous** forcipules

> Large appetite

N
W E
S

SOUTH AMERICA

AMAZON
RAIN FOREST

MAP KEY Giant Centipede
Range

> Range: Within the Amazon
rain forest, although exact range
unknown

> Diet: Crickets, worms, lizards,
toads, mice, bats, small snakes

FUN FACT
Giant centipedes typically
grow up to 12 inches (31 cm)
long. But an 18-inch (46 cm)
specimen was found in
Venezuela!

CREEPY-CRAWLIES

Arthropods have never been popular with humans. People often find scorpions, spiders, and roaches ugly and frightening. Centipedes are no exception. Some people find their many legs and superfast movements terrifying.

The fear of centipedes dates back centuries. In ancient Japan, centipedes were seen as dirty and **impure**. It was thought they were connected to the dead. One Japanese legend describes a centipede the size of a mountain. This monster ate villagers and cattle.

The giant centipede is not as large as a mountain. But this legend may have grown from huge arthropods that roamed Earth long ago. The millipede *Euphoberia* lived

FEAR FACTOR

In the 1800s, Tibetan poet Shabkar reflected on different animals. He wrote about the centipede inspiring fear. "If you enjoy frightening others, you will be reborn as a centipede," Shabkar wrote. Today, there is a special word for the fear of centipedes. It is called *chilopodophobia* (KYE-lo-po-da-fo-be-a).

The Japanese legend about a monstrous centipede is called *Tawara Tōda*, or "My Lord Bag of Rice."

300 million years ago. It was 39 inches (99 cm) long. *Arthropleura*, another millipede, was 8.5 feet (2.6 m) long! Scientists think giant centipedes may have descended from these beasts. The giant centipede is much smaller. But it is the titan of today's centipede species!

FACT MEETS FICTION

Today, scientists estimate there are 8,000 different types of centipede. These centipedes come in a wide range of sizes. Common house centipedes are about one inch (2.5 cm) long. Even though they are so small, many people hate these critters.

There are several types of centipedes often called giant centipedes. *Ethmostigmus rubripes* is one. It is commonly found in Australia, Indonesia, and China. It has a **venomous** bite and can grow more than six inches (15 cm) long.

Scolopendra subspinipes is another species sometimes called giant centipede. It is seven inches (18 cm) long and also venomous. It is found most often in Southeast Asia.

CINEMA-PEDES

Centipedes make an appearance in the 1984 film *Indiana Jones and the Temple of Doom*. In one scene, actress Kate Capshaw gets covered in thousands of bugs. Centipedes crawl up her legs and through her hair. The creepy-crawly actors were not popular with the film's cast and crew.

The giant centipede can be up to 12 times longer than the common house centipede!

At 12 inches (31 cm) long, *Scolopendra gigantea*, or the giant centipede, is the largest known centipede. However, some believe a larger relative called the death crawler exists in the Amazon. People say it is several times the size of the giant centipede. No proof supports this creature's existence. But the giant centipede is sometimes nicknamed death crawler.

MOTHER OF THE YEAR

The giant centipede may have a fearsome reputation. But when caring for young, a giant centipede mother is very protective and devoted. Her motherly duties begin as she prepares to lay eggs.

First, the female giant centipede finds a patch of moist soil or a piece of rotting wood. Then, she lays her eggs. The giant centipede lays many eggs at a time. She coils around them until they hatch. She also grooms her eggs. This keeps them clean and free of mold.

To some animals, such as snakes, centipede eggs are a tasty treat. But the giant centipede will fight to the death to protect her young. She even takes them everywhere she goes. When leaving the nest, the mother centipede tucks the eggs between her many back legs. While walking, she holds her back end up in the air.

Most newly hatched centipedes have fewer legs than adults. They grow more legs over time. The giant centipede is different. It is born with

The stone centipede cares for its eggs just as the giant centipede does. Both coil around their eggs.

all of its legs. But a baby centipede, or larva, still has much growing to do! And in order to grow, the giant centipede must **shed** its **exoskeleton**, also known as its shell. A giant centipede sheds its exoskeleton several times.

Each time it sheds, the centipede must eat something right away. This helps the centipede grow larger before its new shell hardens. Otherwise, the new exoskeleton will harden while it is same size as the centipede's current body. Sometimes, the giant centipede eats its old shell.

The giant centipede larvae grow for several months. During this time, they stick close together. Their mother watches closely over them. Once the larvae can catch their own food, the mother leaves them.

Off on their own, the young giant centipedes don't have busy social lives. They mainly focus on eating and sleeping. Unless one of these centipedes loses a bad fight, each will live for about ten years.

FUN FACT

Centipede means "hundred feet." But most centipedes, including the giant centipede, only have 42 to 46 legs.

A centipede eats its old shell. Until its new exoskeleton hardens, it is very open to attacks from predators.

DAMP, DARK, DEADLY

The giant centipede lives throughout the Amazon rain forest in northern South America. The mysterious **arthropod** seeks out damp, dark places. During the day, it rests beneath rocks, leaves, and rotting logs.

Occasionally, the giant centipede reaches great heights rather than burrowing down low. It is a skillful climber, able to scuttle up tree trunks with ease. This climbing ability is helpful when chasing after prey.

The giant centipede ordinarily emerges at night, when the air is cooler and very moist. The rain forest's wet climate is extremely important to the giant centipede. This is because the giant centipede doesn't drink from puddles or streams. Instead, it obtains its water from the air.

Most arthropod shells are coated in a waxy substance. This keeps them from drying out. But the giant centipede is different. Unlike the average arthropod, it breathes through small holes in its **exoskeleton**. If it were covered in a waxy coating, the centipede would **suffocate**!

The Amazon rain forest covers more than 2.5 million square miles (6.5 million sq km). That's a lot of room for giant centipedes!

While air enters the **exoskeleton**, water makes its way out. Because water is constantly leaving the giant centipede's body, it **dehydrates** easily. So, the giant centipede must be careful to protect itself from the hot sun.

PINCH OF DEATH

The giant centipede is a carnivore. It often eats worms and other insects. But it is not afraid to tackle larger prey. This hungry **arthropod** will also eat toads, lizards, and small birds. The giant centipede has even been observed eating snakes more than nine inches (23 cm) long!

The swift centipede is a fierce hunter. When the sun goes down, it gets right to work. Its eyesight is poor, so it uses its antennae to navigate its surroundings.

When the centipede senses a nearby snack, such as a mouse, it springs into action. Most centipedes are very quick. But the giant centipede is especially known for its fast movements. It is very **flexible** and coils around the mouse in a flash. The centipede latches its legs tightly to the mouse's body. This makes escape quite difficult.

With its victim secure, the giant centipede delivers a death pinch. It uses its front legs to pierce the mouse's neck. But these aren't ordinary legs.

On Australia's Christmas Island, several lizard species are dying out. Researchers believe a type of giant centipede that hunts them is partly to blame.

These specialized limbs are called forcipules. They release a powerful **venom**, killing the mouse within 30 seconds.

The toxic, black-tipped forcipules are found behind the giant centipede's head. A tube runs through each forcipule, ending near the tip.

These tubes contain **venom** glands. When the centipede strikes, these sharp forcipules pierce through the victim's skin. The venom glands then pump out a stream of poison. The mouse becomes **paralyzed**, then dies.

The giant centipede's venom does more than kill the mouse. It also softens the mouse's flesh. This lets the creepy-crawly killer slurp its meal as though it were soup!

The giant centipede also eats bats. While hanging from a cave ceiling, the centipede snags a bat out of the air. It grips the bat with its front legs, then pierces the animal's neck. As the bat dies, the centipede's meal begins.

Researchers were amazed in 2005 when they discovered the giant centipede could eat bats. The giant centipede was the first centipede to exhibit this hunting ability. The centipede's climbing skills were impressive. Its ability to grip the wall while catching bats much heavier than itself was too!

If fearsome forcipules weren't enough, the giant centipede has another natural weapon.

FUN FACT

The giant centipede's forcipules are modified legs that end in sharp claws.

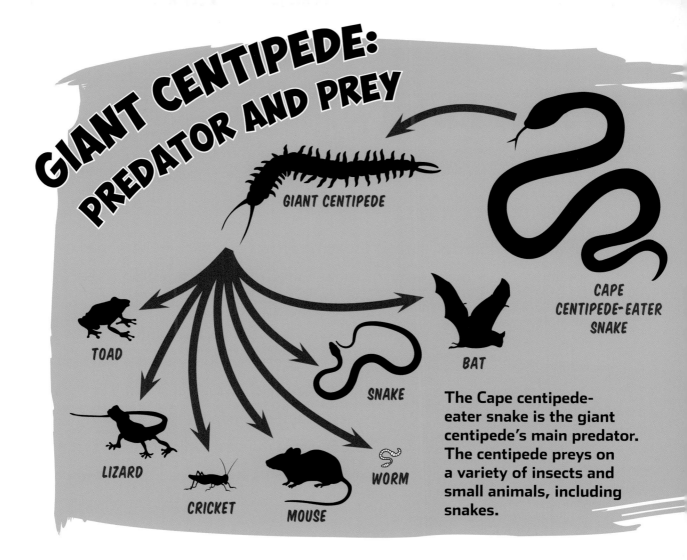

GIANT CENTIPEDE: PREDATOR AND PREY

GIANT CENTIPEDE

CAPE CENTIPEDE-EATER SNAKE

TOAD

BAT

SNAKE

LIZARD

CRICKET

MOUSE

WORM

The Cape centipede-eater snake is the giant centipede's main predator. The centipede preys on a variety of insects and small animals, including snakes.

It **excretes** special chemicals from its many leg joints. These chemicals cause skin **irritation** to other animals that come in contact with the centipede, as well as to humans.

CENTIPEDE VS. SNAKE

Smaller centipedes, such as the common house centipede, have many predators. They make tasty meals for birds, frogs, and **rodents**. These small centipedes are also eaten by other bugs.

Centipedes may even eat each other! Certain centipede larvae eat their mothers after hatching. And if a centipede shows signs of injury or weakness, another centipede may eat it.

But few predators are willing to take on the giant centipede. Its tough shell and **venomous** forcipules make it an unappealing meal. However, one species of snake is always up for the challenge. The Cape centipede-eater snake was named after its favorite meal. Its diet consists mainly of centipedes.

DEADLY BATTLE

In 2013, a team of researchers found a snake and centipede that had both lost a battle. A horn-nosed viper had swallowed a Megarian banded centipede, the giant centipede's close relative. But the centipede clawed its way out of the snake's side! Neither animal survived.

The Cape centipede-eater snake is known for its black head and collar.

The giant centipede is almost twice as wide as the Cape centipede-eater. But the snake's **venom** is even deadlier than that of its creepy-crawly rival. First, the snake kills the giant centipede with a venomous bite. Then it swallows the centipede whole!

HUMAN HAZARDS

Snakes aren't the only creatures that eat huge centipedes. Believe it or not, some humans dine on these creepy critters! The Vietnamese centipede is a type of large centipede. This creature is a popular cooked dish at street markets in Thailand and Vietnam. It is considered a local **delicacy**. And many foreign travelers are thrilled to try it! But how is this **venomous** creature safe to eat?

While cooking, heat breaks down the centipede's venom. But just because it is safe to eat, doesn't mean it's tasty! The Vietnamese centipede is often described as having the taste of a bitter, old clam. Luckily, researchers believe the number of Vietnamese centipedes killed for human food is not high enough to harm its population levels. And *Scolopendra gigantea* has not caught on as a cooked snack at all.

However, humans do threaten the giant centipede population in another way. South America's Amazon rain forest is the largest rain forest

Scorpions, centipedes, insects, and more are sold as snacks at a market stall in Beijing, China.

in the world. But **deforestation** to make room for buildings, farms, and livestock is shrinking the centipedes' home.

The giant centipede's threat level has not been **evaluated** by scientists. So researchers are not certain of its population. But the South American rain forest is key to the giant centipede's survival. As more trees are cleared, the centipede loses both land and food sources. The giant centipede will not last long without prey and proper shelter.

Human actions are threatening to the giant centipede. But these creatures can also be a danger to humans. Their **venom**, which is deadly for its prey, is also harmful to humans. It causes pain, fever, **vomiting**, and weakness in humans. Humans who have been bitten by giant centipedes say the bites are very painful. They compare it to that of a broken bone, or even a gunshot wound.

Although it is painful, adult humans usually survive being bitten. However, small children are not as lucky. In Venezuela, one young boy was killed by a giant centipede bite in 2014.

The centipede's bite is enough to scare most people away from handling one. But some people are more fascinated than frightened. In fact, **exotic** pet dealers have brought the centipede to some US pet stores. These creatures can also be bought online.

HOME INVASION

In 2005, a man in London, England, found a nine-inch (23 cm) giant centipede hiding behind his TV. The man's neighbor was an exotic pet owner and claimed he owned the escaped beast. The Natural History Museum cared for the creature until the neighbor's ownership was made certain.

Giant centipede owners exchange stories, advice, and photos on the Internet.

Remember, researchers have not **evaluated** the giant centipede population. However, they believe the pet trade has not affected giant centipede numbers in the wild. But if pet giant centipedes grow in popularity, their natural populations could become threatened.

NEW DISCOVERIES

There is much humans can learn from the giant centipede. By studying centipede genes, researchers may learn more about how human genes develop. In particular, they may uncover the cause of human **deformities**.

This has to do with the way centipedes' many legs form. Different types of centipedes have different numbers of legs. Each centipede species has a specific pattern of genes. Certain giant centipede genes, called homeoboxes, are also found in humans. Mutations in these genes can cause deformities. By studying genetic mutations between centipede species, researchers could learn about mutations within our own species.

Studying the giant centipede's relatives is also useful to medical researchers. One species, the Chinese red-headed centipede, has **venom** that blocks the **nerve** channels of its prey. Researchers are working to develop painkillers for humans that **mimic** this effect. If successful, the medication will greatly help those suffering from painful conditions.

From fearsome legend, to creepy-crawly pest, to medical marvel. What's next for the giant centipede?

There is still much we can learn from the giant centipede and its relatives. But further research will be impossible unless its rain forest home is preserved. By protecting its **habitat**, we can protect the giant centipede too. Perhaps we will even find its mythical cousin, the death crawler, deep in the jungle.

GLOSSARY

arthropod — a member of the phylum Arthropoda, which includes insects, arachnids, and crustaceans. An arthropod has an exoskeleton and a jointed body and limbs.

deforestation — the act of removing trees and clearing forests.

deformity — a condition in which part of the body does not have the normal or expected shape.

dehydrate — to lose or remove water.

delicacy — a rare or luxurious food.

evaluate — to determine the meaning or importance of something.

excrete — to pass waste material out of the body.

exoskeleton — the outer covering or structure that protects an animal, such as an insect.

exotic — interesting because it is strange or different from the usual.

flexible — able to bend or move easily.

habitat — a place where a living thing is naturally found.

WEBSITES

To learn more about Real Monsters, visit **booklinks.abdopublishing.com**. These links are routinely monitored and updated to provide the most current information available.

impure — unclean.

inject — to forcefully introduce a substance into something.

irritation — the state of being sore or in pain.

mimic — to imitate or copy.

nerve — a bundle of fibers carrying messages between the brain, the spinal cord, and other body parts.

paralyze — to cause a loss of motion or feeling in a part of the body.

rodent — any of several related animals that have large front teeth for gnawing. Common rodents include mice, squirrels, and beavers.

shed — to cast off hair, feathers, skin, or other coverings or parts by a natural process.

suffocate — to die from lack of oxygen.

venom — a poison produced by some animals and insects. It usually enters a victim through a bite or a sting. Something that produces venom is venomous.

vomit — to reject the contents of the stomach out through the mouth.

INDEX